THE SELF-HELP BOOK THEY **DON'T** WANT YOU TO **READ**

Vol. 1

Austin Robinson
& Heath Fowler

Copyright © 2020

11% Happier Publishing House,
in collaboration with

Pothole Press,
an imprint of

AJR Publications

All rights reserved

Cover design by Austin Robinson

First published on Oct. 31st, 2020

ISBN:
978-0-9992029-6-8

Some names and characteristics of people, places, and things have been changed to protect the privacy of the individuals involved.

No part of this book may be reproduced in any form or by any electronic or mechanical means, including information storage and retrieval systems, without permission in writing from the publisher.

Dedicated to You.

ve, Laugh, Love! 50
An Evidence-Based Approach

Respecting The Scam 60
(AKA Relationships)

6. **Pivot to Vulnerability** 79
Learning to Take Off the Mask
and Own Your True Self While
Leaning into the Discomfort
of Shame & Truth

BONUS CONTENT! 90
Fun Leadership Activities!

Empirical Figures Index 106
1.1 – 6.1

About the Authors 115

Content(s)

Publisher's Note — 7

Welcome Home! — 9
Creating a Safe Space, Rent Free

1. **Taking Out The Trash** — 14
   Excreting Negative Self-Talk
   & Hoarding Self-Trash Talk

2. **Getting Over Ur Ex** — 26
   How to Achieve Self-Closure

3. **11% Happier** — 35
   Why Joining a Cult is
   Actually a Good Thing

PUBLISHER'S NOTE

Please, we beg of you, read this book at your own risk. We at AJR Publications and Pothole Press are not held liable for anything that happens to you when you implement the advice given here. Trust us, we have read every page and experimented with every "self-help" guide provided by Austin and Heath on the following pages… and that's all we can say. Legally. We're leaving this ominous note *after* Austin and Heath approved the final draft because we know they won't even buy a copy of their own book. In fact, they didn't apply any of the edits we suggested.

They won't see this, so we implore you to read between the lines and stay safe out there.

- The AJR PUB Team

Welcome Home!
Creating a Safe Space, Rent Free

"Self-help is like a house. It needs a strong foundation, you're required to upkeep it, and it costs a lot of money!"
– Adam Grand, Author of 'Giveth & Taketh'

Welcome to the novel. Feel free to take off your shoes, hang up your coat, and relax into your new literary home. You live here now. A place of peace and tranquility. That'll be $1,350 a month, please! Haha, I'm just kidding. Self-help is free. Creating that loving, caring, happy place inside of you costs nothing, and the pay-out is huge!

As you begin reading this novel, you will start your own personal journey to enlightenment. Originally part of a $50,000 course, the content you find throughout these pages may shock you – you may even feel turned on. This is natural. Our wise words and beautiful philosophies will entice you and ask that you spread your mind wide open. Our advice on your self-help journey will 69 your willpower to create a better life for yourself. Though there is a price tag, what you learn from the content is priceless. However, that price tag is lower than ever.

Now, for the first time ever, we have decided to turn our $50,000 course into a book! For just $4.20! Some of our students have called this a Cheat Sheet Guide to The Second Level of Life. A philosophical evolution, if you will. Our students have altered their way of living to become some of the richest and most successful people on the planet (we won't say who, Bill Gates). Some have begged to pay us $100,000 because they felt the course was simply too cheap for what they got out of it. Actually, we're not even sure why we're going on and on about how amazing and great this content is. Feel free to read a couple reviews from past students and readers for yourself!

"This book will be very, very helpful for me once I take over for my brother, Kim Jung Un."
- Kim Yo Jung

"Dear Heath and Austin, we're sorry, but Orpah Winfrey has decided not to move forward with including your self-help book as part of the O Magazine

2020 Book Club catalogue. She would like for me to forward a message to you both: 'A book of this caliber? It is not simply for the O Magazine Book Club. It is meant for bigger and better things. I would be performing a disservice to both of you by accepting this book into our 2020 catalogue – not to mention that it would overshadow every other book we accept. It is simply too good.' With that, the Orpah Winfrey Team wishes you the best of luck in 2021."

- Orpah Winfrey's employee

"Austin & Heath's Self-Help Course is the sole motive behind my decision to become President of the United States of America, the catalyst of my winning a Nobel Peace Prize, and the reason I am still alive at the age of 96 today!"

- Jimothy Carter

Wow. Just wow. I hope those reviews resonated with you and that you'll consider leaving one when you finish your journey. Namaste.

NOW DIG IN!

Taking Out The Trash
Excreting Negative Self-Talk & Hoarding Self-Trash Talk

"I give each of my employees an hour a day to reflect on their true selves. It's like lunch, but instead of eating food, they eat mindfulness." – Brené Black, Chief Vulnerability Officer

In the recent decade (or maybe before that, who knows) there has been an extensive push to eradicate negative self-talk. The quieting of internal dialogue such as "Don't eat that 5th burrito, you ugly boy" or "You'll never be good enough to eat that" is a movement geared to improve self-esteem. I guess the general idea is to be "nice" to yourself. That's cool and all, and I partially support it. But this ideology limits the innate potential you have. That I have. That WE have. It sucks. It is time we leave room for a new perspective. A new notion that you can indeed talk shit to yourself AND half-heartedly appreciate the garbage you are. Neigh, the garbage you can BE.

Imagine you walk into a room with dim lighting and something someone decided to call art. Everyone in this room is pretending to be funny and talking about philosophy or how their parents don't give them enough money. Now open your eyes! Yes, you are at an art show. The pretentious aroma of essential oil lubed beards punches your stupid face. You can't help but feel out of place. *I'm not good enough to be here! What the fuck is art!? Why does it always suck and judge my mortal ass!?*

Stop here. You are in the midst of a serious dilemma. You are about to forfeit yourself to negative self-talk in a situation where you are prompted to feel inferior. You are out of place, and they know it. AND they want your uncultured ass to know it. Feeling this is valid and inevitable, as these shit stain events are meant to do this. But shut your ungrateful ass up and listen. Creating the internal dialogue that you are unworthy to this <u>specific</u> event is the path of least resistance, and it is unhealthy, my friend.

So what then? Tell myself how great I am and how much I deserve to be present here? ABSOLUTELY NOT! You are not great, and you have never been great. But here is the key: roll with it and generalize it. That is the difference, importance, and radical power of self-trash talk. I define Self-Trash Talk as this: "An empowering form of negative self-talk that assumes you are a small piece of existence that has never been worthy or deserving of anything, and therefore results in personal and existential freedom."

Heavy, I know. Just like you, you dumpster baby. Ok, back to this shitty analogy. So how does your self-trash talk manifest in this unrelatable fart show scenario? Well, if you remember, you were at a point where you were gonna look in a mirror and talk shit. I'm not only telling you to continue, but to embrace it. Yes, you aren't as smart as these people. And yes, you will never be able to appreciate beauty. But guess what? YOU ARE FUCKING TRASH, and goddamn it, don't let them forget it.

That is the true difference between negative self-talk and self-trash talk. You own your shitty flaws, communicate them with yourself, and don't give a fuck. Some schools of thought say to love your trash qualities. Honestly, that's overrated. You can and probably should be ashamed. But in the face of whatever emotion comes, you must take the burden of your garbage existence and wear it like a crown. A trash crown made of used condoms and poopie. Embracing the trash leads to revolutionary bliss.

An issue some folks have with this paradigm shift is that it leads to self-hate. I define self-hate as: You should. But the caveat is the way this manifests and the outcome it produces. Look at the following empirical model I shitted together:

Negative Self-Talk → Self-Hatred → Spiritual Death

Look familiar? Yeah, same. This is the natural course of events when Negative Self-Talk takes hold. The narrative becomes toxic, and baby you're slipping under. But watch THIS:

Negative Self-Talk → Self-Trash Talk → Slop → Garbage Truck → Cow Shit → Spiritual Enlightenment

Ok, open your eyes again. Do you see what just happened there?? When you simply let negative self-talk exist, it results in self-hatred and then eventually spiritual death. But when self-trash talk is used as an input to mitigate negative self-talk, you eventually follow a path to spiritual enlightenment.

Please turn to the next page to see these models applied to a diagram in action.

Figure 1.1

So, if you couldn't understand my diagram because you are not a visual learner (I respect that, we are all unique), let me explain further. Self-trash talk cannot lead to self-hatred because it redirects the perceptions produced by negative self-talk. You reshape your mean words into mean, undeniable truths. The truths cannot be adjusted, and why should they be? You stare down your dumpster lifestyle and accept it. You are your trash AND your treasure, and you do not need to alter yourself because you simply are.

Now keep your eyes closed. Let's play around with how we can use the above models to reach dank scum existence.

1) "I really wish someone would date me and have wild animal sex with me, but I am too ugly." **(A)**

This will be our "A" input: an example of negative self-talk. Referencing our first model, we know this will result in self-hatred. That will most likely look like this:

2) "I hate my ugly ass with a passion and everyone should hate me just as much if not more

and I will most certainly never get laid in the butt." **(B)**

The above statement reflecting self-hatred will be our moderating variable "B".

So, when A leads to B we get our C. The big C looks like this:

3) "My life has no purpose, I have no connection to anyone, and I must live out my wasted self until I face a boring death." **(C)**

Yikes! Look at this Debby Downer! But alas, A → B → C.

OK, so let's try something a bit different. We keep our A, but let's insert a different moderating variable. One I call 'Self-Trash Talk', which will be our big "D."

4) "LOL FUCK IT IM UGLY AF AND REPULSIVE SUCK MY NASTY PEEN." **(D)**

Well, now! I feel refreshed already! But wait, there's more. When A instead leads to D, our model looks like this:

A → D

So, let's just go ahead and put it all together! We end up with:

A → D → @ → % → :p → G

Please turn to the next page to see this formula in action.

"I really wish someone would date me and have wild animal sex with me, but I am too ugly."

'A' variable

"I hate my ugly ass with a passion and everyone should hate me just as much if not more and I will most certainly never get laid in the butt."

'B' variable

"My life has no purpose, I have no connection to anyone, and I must live out my wasted self until I face a boring death."

'C' variable

"LOL FUCK IT IM UGLY AF AND REPULSIVE SUCK MY NASTY PEEN."

'D' variable

'Dark Scam Existence' Model

A → B → C

'Dank Scum Existence' Model

A → D → @ → % → :p → G

Figure 1.2

You are likely feeling waves of emotions after seeing that, and I want you to know I see you and that they are valid. As you can tell, G is spiritual enlightenment. It manifests as follows:

5) "Cool, guess I'll masturbate, heat up a lean cuisine, watch Friday Night Lights, and pass out." **(G)**

You see that? You FEEL that? That is the exceptional power of self-trash talk. It reaffirms that you are worthless and encourages spiritual indulgence. Restraints retire and new possibilities proliferate. I would say Nirvana, but I feel like that's appropriative and something this conversation is generally unworthy of.

Getting Over Ur Ex
How to Achieve Self-Closure

"The very first thing I tell my students is to cook a soup out of their discomfort. Sprinkle in some fear and shame. Lean into the imperfections at medium heat. Then throw in a shit ton of self-help!" – Sheryl Sandman, Leaner

How many times have you been going out with a boy (or girl or enby or whatever you're into, I literally don't care. At all.) and he ghosts you in the middle of your relationship? It has happened to me at least four times. Anyway, it sucks! We all know that feeling. Wouldn't it be great if there were some way to achieve closure all by yourself? Without having to rely on the responsibility of someone who told you they'd love you forever and that you can have your wedding catered by Chili's? Me too.

That's why a famous psychologist came up with 5 simple steps towards self-closure. Titled "AJR's Hierarchy of Getting Over Your Ex," this pyramid-esque structure contains everything you need to know in order to start being yourself again and stop eating ice cream sandwiches at the same time every day. I'm ecstatic, too. Pictured on the next page is what psychology students will see in their textbooks one day.

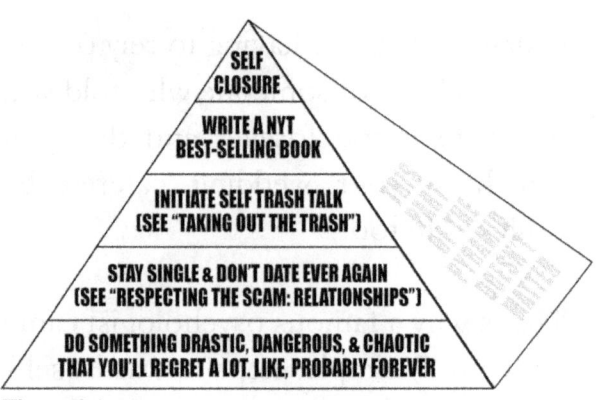

Figure 2.1

Wow! Now that's neat! I can't wait to climb the pyramid and feel at peace with the fact that someone decided to wake up one day and not love me anymore! Not to mention, it looks like I might get my steps in with this climb (ha-ha)! NO. This pyramid is not for climbing – it's for gradual *lifting*. You will be lifted up through the sections of this pyramid, and you know who will be lifting you up? You. We'll go from the bottom to the top, where you want to end up.

Do Something Drastic, Dangerous, & Chaotic That You'll Regret A Lot. Like, Probably Forever

Now, this initial section might seem counterproductive. *Why am I impulsively reacting to such a negative situation – shouldn't I be taking care of myself and talking it out with friends?* Sure, if you want to be among the minority of people who actually do that. Most people make very rash and life-ruining decisions immediately after a break-up, and that means it's probably the best thing to do. It's the storm before the calm, right? Or whatever. Try immediately hooking up with four other people all in one night or hiring a hacker to shut down your ex's Facebook and Instagram accounts. The possibilities are literally endless!

The more and longer you regret your actions, the quicker you get lifted up the pyramid!

Stay Single And Don't Date Ever Again (See Chapter 5: "Respecting The Scam")

What got you into this mess in the first place? What brought you to this theory about a pyramid and a hierarchy of blah blah blah. Dating did! What the heck, why did you do that!? Well, I guess we live, and we learn. And the primary lesson taken from whatever messed up thing your ex did to you is probably to eliminate any possibility of it ever happening again. Directly after making bad decisions, go into your phone and delete every contact of whoever you happen to be attracted to. And if you don't want to waste the energy, just delete all of your contacts! A relationship can strike at any point, and you don't want to fall victim to another trip on this pyramid, do you? If you never date again, you'll always be at the top!

Initiate Self Trash Talk (See Chapter 1: "Taking Out The Trash")

Heath put it perfectly when he told you to turn negative self-talk into self-trash talk! After getting lifted up through bad decisions and becoming relationally abstinent, you are going to want to scream at yourself and question why you even like you – in a bad way. Don't do this! Instead, do it in a *good* way. "I am literally the reason why population control should exist" sounds so much better with a smile on your face! You will enthusiastically thank yourself for the amazing ability to believe that dumpsters look more like home than actual houses. The quicker you start loving the way you put yourself down, the quicker you can arrive at the next section of the pyramid.

Write A *New York Times* Best-Selling Book

Yes, you will need to completely write, edit, and publish a book that has to make it onto the *New York Times* Bestsellers List before you can even achieve self-closure. Sorry! But don't worry, because once you've made a couple of terrible mistakes, sworn off all the greasy bats known as "significant others," and accepted your fate as a trash-human, it will be so easy for you to sit down and talk about your experiences following your breakup. No one cares about groundbreaking science or investigative journalism pieces on human rights violations – it's all about you! Your book will most likely be a hit because no one actually cares about anything of substance anymore!

<u>Self-Closure</u>

FINALLY! Oh, brother, was that a journey! I'm so glad it's over and I can go home to my family that I haven't seen in a month. BUT WAIT. It's not over. Once you've traversed the cemented memories of your ex that make up the walls of this pyramid, you need to ensure you stay at the top. If you can stand the cold and lonely space that is the peak of this structure, you can receive closure on just about anything you can imagine. Didn't get the frozen yogurt flavor you wanted from your favorite FroYo store because they were out? Oh well! That doesn't even matter to you! You got over it before it even presented itself as a problem! Wow. Your ex has nothing on you.

Now that you're over your ex, I guess there's no reason to continue this anymore! You're welcome! Bye-bye!

11% Happier
Why Joining a Cult is Actually a Good Thing

"11 is better than 10. Even I know that." – Dave Harris

It was a Friday afternoon. I was making my way downtown, walking fast; faces were passing, and I was homebound. Now, this wasn't unusual from the majority of my days walking home in Portland – the Vitamin D Deficiency capital of the world. In fact, that was the problem: it was exactly like the day before it, and the day before that, and the day before that, and the subordinate clause before this. I was growing weary and tired of the day-in and day-out of it all! I direly needed to change things up. I had tried macro-dosing on LSD (i.e. when you do a large amount of it), hiring a flash-mob (but instead of dancing, they spontaneously clapped as they followed me around), and committing a Class A Felony (unrelated). I even tried yoga. Nothing was working! And then, I met someone who changed my life forever…

Sound familiar? I know you can relate, you boring piece of shining gold. 9 out of 11 adults consider their lives incredibly dull. It's gotten so bad that we have to make up fake statistics just to feel anything. But what if I told you there is a tried and true way to discover everyday happiness and excitement? What if I told you that a formula was recently discovered to not only determine your scientific level of enjoyment in life, but also explain how you can exponentially increase said enjoyment? Okay well let me finish my flashback, asshole (jk ☺) (NOT ☹) *airhorn noises*

Just as I turned the corner past the downtown Macy's, a ghastly figure donning a red robe appeared on the sidewalk in an ethereal manner. I walked right past it because I was NOT about to deal with that. I went into the nearby corner store for my daily dose of Funyuns© and ham. After walking around the store pretending I was going to buy anything other than Funyuns and ham, I decided to check out. I gave the cashier $11.11 and headed out the door. That's when a Man with a vape pen in one hand and a sense of confidence in the other approached me.

"How would you like to be 11% Happier?" the Man said. It was a question, but He said it with such conviction that it presented itself as a statement.

I couldn't help but hang on every word, every syllable, every letter of His question. I thought to myself, *I would like to be 11% happier.* But my mouth said, "Tell me more."

Next thing I know, I was sitting in a convention chair at a self-help retreat in southern California with 200 other attendees. It's almost as if I was teleported 15 hours down south by the promise of becoming "11% Happier." To be honest, I still didn't know what that meant, and I had no recollection of anything since I bought those Funyuns and ham. *Did I even eat them?* I thought to myself before the same Man who enticed me there entered the stage in front of us.

"HELLLOOOOOOO 11 Percenters! LET ME HEAR YOU MAKE SOME NOISE!"

The crowd around me went wild. A cacophony of positive *whoop*s and *yeah*s entered my ears as I used my other senses to figure out what the hell was going on. I noticed some marketing signs on either side of the Man that said, "The 11% Happier Retreat. Now with 11% more retreat." I was trying to work out what that meant when the people around me began doing the 'Crowd Wave', which I completely messed up for my row. As the people on either side of me made nasty faces in my direction for ruining their moment, the rest of room started chanting, "1 PLUS 1 EQUALS 11!" *I'm not sure about that,* I thought to myself before the Man continued.

"I have seen the future for each and every one of you. And I gotta say: it is fantastic! It is 11% Happier! I understand why you're here... you are sick and tired of waking up only to go to work, only to go back home again. All of you deserve better than that. You deserve to be 11% Happier! When was the last time you went after what you wanted? What you desired? When was the last time someone told you that you're better than that dead-end office job you go back to year after year?

When was the last time you were 11% Happier!?"

He keeps saying that phrase over and over again. I'm not sure this speech has much substance, but He's definitely striking a chord.

"Welcome to the 11% Happier Retreat, hosted by the 11% Happier Cult. That's right – we aren't afraid of the term *Cult* here. You will spend the next 11 days realizing your future, going after what you deserve, and truly becoming 11% Happier. Well, if that's a cult, then a cult doesn't sound half bad!"

Laughter came from the other attendees as I tried to reckon with how I possibly went from buying salty onion-flavored chips and meat to accidentally joining a cult that appeared to be obsessed with the number 11.

"Now, a couple of my people will walk around the room and hand you your retreat clothing. These individuals are known as SIREs, and they have achieved not only an 11% Happier living, but also Superspiritual™ Independence – so much so, that they have Retired Early from the working life you know so well. Once you have your retreat clothing, head to your Enlightenment Quarters and change. You have a long 11 days ahead of you. Remember our slogan: *Vulnerability. Enlightenment. Freedom. Pivot To Us.*"

"May we lean in and pivot to you," several attendees responded to the Man, whose name I still didn't know. I would later discover these attendees were "Returners" or "12 Percenters" and were attempting to reach the next level of happiness: 12% Happier.

I began walking back to my hotel room, which was just oddly referred to as my "Enlightenment Quarters" as if we weren't inside a LaQuinta Inn. All of the garments were bright red and had "Ask me how you can be 11% Happier!" printed on them, like our mission was to convert the other hotel patrons during our stay. I quickly put them on and headed to the dining room for what I was told was a game of "Lean, Lean, Pivot." It was described to me in a way that reminded me of Duck, Duck, Goose, but the SIRE I spoke with seemed confused when I compared the two.

When we were all huddled inside of the dining room – which the Retreat had strangely titled the 'Vulnerability Realm' – we were told the SIREs were about to pass around something called "New Caffeine." We were assured that the Cult does not believe in coffee, but this is as far as they went in describing the mysterious drink. As they handed me a cup, a foul smell hit my nose and a dark yellow hue entered my vision. We were instructed to consume the New Caffeine three times a day for the duration of the retreat in order to bring ourselves closer to what was known as the "Superspiritual Consciousness."

Suddenly, the Man entered the Vulnerability Realm and a hush fell over the crowd. "Now that you have consumed The New Caffeine and leaned into contract with your eventual Superspiritual Consciousness, it's time to teach you the HappinessFormula™

so that you, too, can reach an 11% Happier way of living. Let's begin…"

Well, reader, I bet you thought I was about to give you free content on how to actually become 11% Happier! Fat chance, you Unenlightened Worldling! But if you truly want to achieve an 11% Happier existence like I did, simply fill out the membership form on the next page and place it in an envelope with 11% of your monthly take-home pay from work. To retain membership, you must consistently commit to this monthly 11% income tithe. Otherwise, your Happiness Level will not increase, and you will go back to your boring, poopy life, you shit.

The 11% Happier Cult
Membership Form

1. Pre-Tax Income:_____

2. Bank Account #:_____

3. Full Name:_____

4. Do you want to achieve Superspiritual Consciousness?   **Yes**   **No**

5. Residential Address:_____

6. Where you spend most of your time?
   _____

7. Do we have permission to kidnap you?
   Yes   [no 2nd option]

8. Social Security Number:____-___-_____

9. Please list 11 people we can recruit:

   1._____ 2._____ 3._____ 4._____

   5._____ 6._____ 7._____ 8._____

   9._____ 10._____ 11._____

10. Would you like to be 11% Happier™?
    Yes!   **I Elect 12%+**

11. Signature:_____   Date:_____

The
11% Happier Cult
Disclosure Agreement

1. By signing the 'Membership Form', you agree to let us take at least 11% of your pre-taxed income every month - unless you designate a higher percentage for more Happiness. Each percentage point you elect past 11 increases your Happiness Formula possibility by 1, for a maximum possibility of 100% Happiness.

2. By providing your Bank Account Number(s), you agree to let us authorize an ACH transaction, described in Clause 1. You may choose to provide us with a Checking, Savings, or Retirement Account. If you choose the latter, please make us your Benefactor on the account(s).

3. You need to provide us with your full name: First, Middle (if applicable), and Surname. Additionally, we need to know any previous names you used to go by, even if you are in the Witness Protection Program. By providing your name, you agree to let us conduct the Background Check outlined in Clause 8.

4. Superspiritual Consciousness is defined as not only achieving your 11% Happier goal, but also becoming Spiritually Independent and Retiring Early from your working life. The individuals who achieve Superspiritual Consciousness are considered SIREs. Of course, because it is not possible for us to take 11% or more of your pre-taxed income if you are not working, Superspiritual Consciousness is only allowed for members who have successfully recruited at least 11 new cult members.

5 & 6. You are required to provide us with the physical address in which you reside, as well as every place where you spend most of your time (please consider adding which times during the day you are located at these locations). These will help us when we conduct your Kidnapping, outlined in Clause 7.

7. The 11% Happier Cult affectionately refers to your Kidnapping as "The Unmasking". However, we were told by Law Enforcement that we are not legally allowed to refer to it as anything other than "Kidnapping." Once your membership application has been processed and the closest SIRE has conducted your Background Check - referenced in the Clause 8 - you will be Kidnapped anytime within the 11th week from the membership application submission date. Please leave that week open.

8. By providing your Social Security Number (or Social Insurance Number, if in Canada), you agree to let us conduct The Background Check on you. While not officially recognized by the governments of any nations we have offices in, our Background Check works for us. You will need to mail us your fingerprints, a lock of your hair, a tube of your saliva, and a tooth (any work) within one week of submitting your application so the Kidnapping can be conducted on time.

9 & 10. As referenced in Clause 4, you will need to provide us with at least 11 referrals of people you want us to recruit on your behalf. You can provide more if you would like, as that would only increase your chances of achieving SIRE status and 11%+ Happiness!

11. Please sign and date your application, and good luck!

Great! Once The Directors have received your Initiative Currency™ (what we call money), you will be sent a Welcome Packet filled with the tools and supplements you'll need to be 11% Happier. And yes, you will receive the HappinessFormula algorithm and calculations that were created by none other than Him.

Next step: It's incredibly important for you to have 11 people in mind to tell about the 11% Happier Cult. The more people you get signed up, the more Underlings you'll have and the higher your Happiness Level increases! Every Underling your Underlings sign up gets added to your Paradigm Ladder™. All of the logistics will be explained in the HappinessFormula. Once you and your Underlings complete initiation, you will have the opportunity to become an

Enlightenment Consultant™, which gives you exclusive access to additional Happiness Percentages. After all, 12 Percenters do have more fun! And don't even get me started on 13 Percenters.

I look forward to working with you on your future. Soon, you too will become 11% Happier.

See you at the annual Pivoting.

. . . .
.𝔙 u l n e r a b i l i t y.
.𝔈 n l i g h t e n m e n t.
.𝔉 r e e d o m.
.𝔓 i v o t 𝔗 o 𝔘 s.
.w w w . 1 1 p e r c e n t . o r g.

Live, Laugh, Love!
An Evidence-Based Approach

"For years we didn't understand the science behind Live, Laugh, Love. After decades of research, we finally have an answer." – Mary Condo, Self-Diagnosed Tidier

Abstract

The age-old question: What is the meaning of life? Well, I cannot answer that. The data is not in. But maybe we can explore a parallel quandary: What is the secret to happiness? Fortunately, this can be answered. After centuries of polling and analysis, this data *is* in. It is in and it is unapologetic. The secret is… how can we put this… a non-secret. It is not a hypothesis or a theory. It is <u>law</u>.

And that law is: LIVE, LAUGH, LOVE.

The trials, the case studies, the sacrifices (actual lives lost, RIP), and the stuff have all gotten us here. Live. Laugh! Love? We know beyond a shadow of a doubt that this is the answer to happiness, but we are still unearthing the execution. The tangible practice remains elusive. UNTIL NOW. Because I solved it using a big brain and a lot of reading. Like all academics, I retreated from the actual realities of the world so I could bring you a lot of words. It is as proven as anything else, and if you disagree you are probably not smart. That's academia, and I did not make those rules.

We will begin by defining each of the three components that comprise the LLLLaw – the metric abbreviation for Live, Laugh, Love. First up, we have "Live." The definition of Live according to Google is to stay alive. Next up, "Laugh." The Marriam Webster's Dictionary defines Laugh as "to make the spontaneous sounds and movements of the face and body that are the instinctive expressions of lively amusement and sometimes also of contempt or derision." "Love" is the trickiest to define. I've never been in love or been loved. That's academia for you! Scholars have best summarized Love as feeling lots of good stuff towards [x] (insert anything). Once we unpack Love further in this academic article, I think we will feel more confident on how this actually manifests.

Now that we have clearly defined each of LLLLLaw's individual components, we can critically explore how to implement the science. I want to dissect the pieces so you have the tools to obtain this enlightened state. Before getting into the gold (and I know, the part you are paying for), we need some ground rules:

> 1). Don't question anything.
>
> 2). Do exactly as I say.

Now you're basically in academia too! Let's enter the world of Live, Laugh, Love together!

<u>Dictum Primis: Live</u>

The easiest of our trinity. OR IS IT!? To reach an enlightened state of Live, you must do only one thing: NOT DIE. This might sound impossible, and unfortunately it is with the technology out right now. Four out of five people will die, and there is not much we can do about it. We can tip the scales in our favor with some simple techniques:

> 1). Do not leave your house EVER. Just don't do it. Studies have shown that a lot of people

die outside of their house. *The term house refers to any place you live, including a box or a hole*

2). Prevent murder. Get a sword and some serious surveillance equipment installed around your house. Don't let "them" in.

3). Get a lot of buttons that you can push to alert emergency services to come. AND PUSH THEM. When in doubt, push it out!

4). Eat healthy meals and exercise.

5). Follow some of the above, but ultimately you may need to build a bunker. Something that is impervious to nuclear war and /or other bombs. Adjust as required.

Follow these five steps and you will probably not die! *The author of this cannot account for all pre-existing conditions or other things that result in death ☹*

Dictum Dos: Laugh

I actually think this one is harder than Live. And studies show I am right! It is hard to constantly laugh, and the exact quality of laughter required is still in the beta phase of clinical trials. It is hypothesized that full belly laughter is far superior to the chuckle, but unfortunately there is a link between cancer and hardcore laughter. I think a middle ground is required here, and we will call this the "Standard Laugh," or SL for short. Just give a good old-fashioned laugh and you are probably there.

Now keep doing it. Forever.

Some folks really struggle on the fourth day, but persistence is key. Anytime you cramp up or start crying, shut your baby face up and keep laughing. Studies show that 2/3 people keep laughing after that marker, AND experience intensive psychosis. Just don't give up!

Dicktum Threesome: Love

Finally… we have come to the most difficult and controversial of the LLLLLLLLLLaws. "Love" is not as tangible as the above… until now! Thank god for science! Just kidding, what god? Because science! Love is actually really easy to obtain if you distill it to the most basic mathematical formula. I will present it here:

$X=Y$
$Y=ABC$
$ABC=WQ+JKLMAO^4$
↠⇛⇐≣⇐↘∩ - Q= <(._.<)

Take the quadratic formula of pie and multiply it by 11, and…
10=LOVE

Dictum Primus: LIVE
To reach the enlightened state of LIVE, simply don't die! Follow these techniques to not die: NEVER leave your house, get a sword and surveillance equipment, alert emergency services all the time, eat healthy meals and exercise, and build a bunker!

Dictum Dos: LAUGH
Through a complex algorithm, figure out the exact quantity and quality of LAUGHter you need. While full belly laughter is superior to the chuckle, there is a link to cancer with hardcore laughter. It's best to use SL: Standard Laughter. Now do this constantly forever!

Dicktum Threesome: LOVE
X=Y   Y=ABC   ABC=WQ+JKLMAO^4   ▒▒▒▒▒▒ − Q= <(._.<)
Quadratic Formula of Pie * 11   **10=LOVE**

Figure 4.1

I know that not everyone is a scholar, so I'll do my best to dumb this down. Love is literally a lie! And that's what actually makes it so easy. All you have to do is tell yourself and others that you Love! For example, this is why people make statements like, "If we all just loved each other, everything would be fine" or "Love people despite them being a bad person." Obviously, these statements make no sense. Or when people say they love Sprite™? Or the TV where they say nerd things and boonga banga and a fake audience laughs. Who loves that? Someone lying, that's who.

In fact, there is some evidence to suggest that engaging in too much love is contraindicated with emotional instability, commitment issues, and caffeine. Use at your own risk!

In Conclusion…
Don't die, laugh on loop for eternity, and lie through your stupid, laughing

teeth. Happiness is that easy, friends. And that's on the <u>evidence</u>!

Respecting The Scam
(AKA Relationships)

"The ultimate #LifeHack is going to a thrift store, buying a $1.00 pair of pants, and then selling them to rich people at a 10,000% mark-up." – Sophie Russo, Thrifter Grifter

What's up with dating? What is it? It's weird and everyone seems to be doing it. But why? Literally why? Our emotionally paralyzing loneliness? Societal grooming? Just for the hell of it? I'm trying to understand it, but the only thing that there is to understand is this: <u>dating is a scam</u>.

That's right, folks! Relationships and dating are just one big scam on par with that of pyramid schemes and Enron. Oh, you don't remember Enron? The world's biggest economic scandal ever? The situation that was made into a play by a British playwright, and almost into a musical by me, Austin Robinson? Well, you don't really need to know about it for reference because if you think about dating, you're basically 99% of the way there.

Here's what I mean: Relationships are ever-changing and require us to dissect them and apply new-age philosophies to them CONSTANTLY. And half of the time, they aren't even real… Have you ever heard of Catfishing? Catfishing is the act of becoming an entirely different person to someone who has romantic aspirations for and expectations of your fake persona. You could guide and execute an entire relationship online without even giving away any of your real information. Now that's what I call a scam! Try it out sometime and tell me that isn't the most Enron shit that has ever happened.

Actually, now that I think about it, I want to give you telltale signs that you're being scammed, and also tips on how to scam someone else.

HOW TO TELL IF YOU'RE BEING SCAMMED:

- Are you or a loved one currently in a relationship or looking to pursue dating?

- Have you often asked, "What are all of these apps for?" while looking at the App Store on your iPhone and realizing that there's a new dating app every single day?

- Has anyone ever "asked you out" or have you ever run into a stranger who has asked you to get "drinks" with them?

- Are you currently in a 15-year-long marriage with your best friend and love every second of it?

- Flowers?

If any of the above bullet points apply to you, then sorry: you're being scammed. My expert scientific advice is to promptly reevaluate everything you're doing and probably start your life over. Sorry! Dating is on par with identity theft, and that means that you need to basically get a new identity. Unfortunate. However, there are ways you can scam other people with "dating."

HOW TO SCAM SOMEONE ELSE:

- Identify someone you really like and then ask them to go on a date.

- Marry ur high school sweetheart.

- Unconditionally be there for the human being you call your "significant other" no matter what.

- Agree to go on a date from a popular dating app.

- Pull a 35-year-long emotional heist that ends in marriage with your soulmate.

You're about ready to enter the world and scam a couple of people! I'm really proud of you, and I wish you the best of luck. Remember: the longer the relationship lasts, the more of a scandal it is.

But before you go, let's continue outlining just how ridiculous dating is. One thing I find funny and exposing about dating and Enron is how similar their Wikipedia pages are. I mean just look at them side to side:

Enron's Wikipedia Page

Enron

From Wikipedia, the free encyclopedia

This article is about the corporation. For the play, see Enron (play).

Enron Corporation was an American energy, commodities, and services company based in Houston, Texas. It was founded in 1985 as the result of a merger between Houston Natural Gas and InterNorth, both relatively small regional companies. Before its bankruptcy on December 2, 2001, Enron employed approximately 20,000 staff and was one of the world's major electricity, natural gas, communications and pulp and paper companies, with claimed revenues of nearly $101 billion during 2000.[1] *Fortune* named Enron "America's Most Innovative Company" for six consecutive years.

At the end of 2001, it was revealed that its reported financial condition was sustained by institutionalized, systematic, and creatively planned accounting fraud, known since as the Enron scandal. Enron has since become a well-known example of willful corporate fraud and corruption. The scandal also brought into question the accounting practices and activities of many corporations in the United States and was a factor in the enactment of the Sarbanes–Oxley Act of 2002. The scandal also affected the greater business world by causing the dissolution of the Arthur Andersen accounting firm.[2]

Enron Corporation

Enron logo
Former type	Public
Traded as	NYSE: ENE
Industry	Energy
Fate	Bankruptcy
Predecessor	InterNorth (Northern Natural

Dating's Wikipedia Page

Dating

From Wikipedia, the free encyclopedia

Dating was an American energy, commodities, and services company based in Houston, Texas. It was founded in 1985 as the result of a merger between Houston Natural Gas and InterNorth, both relatively small regional companies. Before its bankruptcy on December 2, 2001, Enron employed approximately 20,000 staff and was one of the world's major electricity, natural gas, communications and pulp and paper companies, with claimed revenues of nearly $101 billion during 2000.[1] Fortune named Enron "America's Most Innovative Company" for six consecutive years.

Relationships	
Types	[show]
Activities	[show]
Endings	[show]
Emotions and feelings	[show]
Practices	[show]
Abuse	[show]

v · T · E

At the end of 2001, it was revealed that its reported financial condition was sustained by institutionalized, systematic, and creatively planned sexual relations. This period of courtship is sometimes seen as a precursor to engagement or marriage.[1][2] Some cultures require people to wait until a certain age to begin dating, which has been a source of controversy.

Do you see it??????????????????????

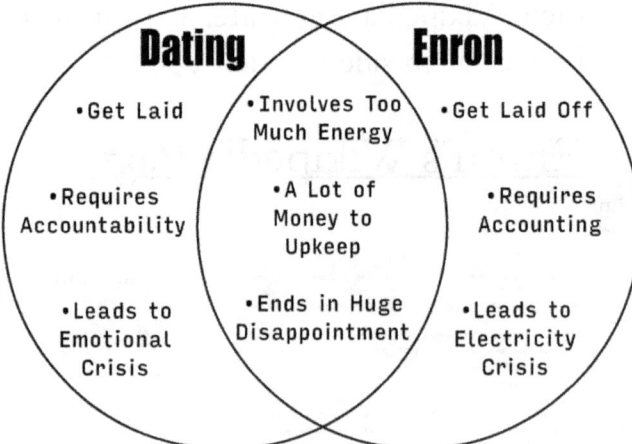

Figure 5.1

I know what you're thinking: *But Austin, if my entire love life is just one big scam, then how am I supposed to ever find someone to love, or know if my significant other is just scamming me?* Well, to answer your first question: if dating is a scam, then you can't possibly believe in love. That's weird. And to answer your second question: the scamming is always happening no matter what. You're gonna have to break up with your significant other. UNLESS. That's right – there is a way to keep the love of your life in your life and also acknowledge that it's a complete sham. If you don't want to live in a world filled with fake relationships and scandals, you're gonna have to delete love altogether. However, you can just do what most people do: ignore the fact that relationships are a scam, and just continue on with the one you love. If you choose this option but you are single, that means you will continue to use dating apps. In that case, you're going to need further advice on how to be completely indifferent to the fact that every romantic relationship around you is fabricated.

Now this section is only for people who are single and, thus, haven't been infected with the delusion that dating is real and not a con. So, if you currently have the virus, then stop reading this chapter. Just read these three words for the next 10 minutes: YOU'RE RIGHT, DATING IS REAL. YOU ARE NOT IN A STATE OF MISCONCEPTION ABOUT THE IDEA OF DATING AND RELATIONSHIPS. GOOD JOB. YOU'RE DOING WELL!

There are three levels, if you will, of

dating that you must go through in order to find someone to scam effectively. They are: 1). Creating an account on a dating app, 2). Planning the perfect first date, and 3). Serial dating so you can scam as many people as possible. Let's start with Level 1.

Level 1: Dating Apps

Dating is a form of art, and the dating app is your canvas! Get ready to paint! First, you need to download a dating app – any will do. Next, you need to think of a bio (short for "biography") for your dating profile. A bio is something everyone will see, so it needs to represent you – or, you know, not at all. Here are a couple of bios that I have used for myself in the past:

1) In prison. If you want to meet me, you have to give them my ID number. It's #002481. Don't

tell them I have a phone in here – just say you're my brother or something.

2) Looking for a drinking partner! And my parents. Where are my parents ☹

3) Check out my website! www.pornhub.com

4) I'm not bi, so why would I have a bio............

5) Thank you for visiting my dating profile! How was your trip? Can I get you anything? Maybe a cup of tea or a snack? I got some Whales in t- Oh, Whales? They're sort of like Goldfish, but a different bran- Oh, okay. Yeah, just the tea? Well, make yourself at home!

6) Hi! Name is Austin. I love hiking, dogs, and traveling. Let's grab a beer or two! Let's get several beers. Let's get drunk on beer. Let's buy a brewing machine together. Let's rob a beer distillery. Let's get so drunk on beer that we burn down a liquor store. Let's die in that fire while covered in beer. Cheers! Message me and get to know me!

Level 2: The Perfect First Date

Once you've filled out your bio and profile, you can now start chatting with other individuals. People on dating apps typically have the brainpower of a 5-year-old, so don't expect too many conversations that last beyond "Hi!" and "Nothing much." But for those times that the stars align and you do chat with someone who knows what a book is, you will want to plan the perfect first date. And that's where I come in. I'll be your personal dating concierge and first date curator. Here are some first date examples:

1) Have him take you to the collective funeral of 12 different first responders who died fighting an explosion. Make sure every U.S. President (pre-2016) except for Bill Clinton is in attendance. This will make him fall in love with you and then leave you two years later, guaranteed!

2) Go to Chili's and order the 2 for $25 (yes, it was only $20 five years ago, but then inflation happened) together to save money. Make this a tradition so

that when y'all eventually break up, you continue to order it for yourself and spread it over the next four meals.

3) Visit IKEA to rip-off the movie <u>500 Days of Summer</u> by pretending to be a married couple shopping for furniture. Only, instead of falling in love, make sure he absolutely hates your guts within a six-month timeframe. Then watch Finding Dory together afterwards.

4) Take him to the house you grew up in and introduce him to every single one of your close family members. That way, when he ghosts you in the middle of your relationship, it's really awkward for the whole family.

Level 3: Rinse & Repeat

Yay! You did it! You created a dating profile on your cell phone, you went on a date the movies will be writing about until the end of time, and you ended it! All in a day's work. Make sure you continue this hard, but necessary, work by becoming a serial dater. That's right: rinse and repeat what you just did. Make it a game! See how many people you and your friends can date. It's kind of like being back in middle school. In fact, this philosophy is widely known as *The Ancient Middle School Courtship System of Hyperspeed Serial Dating*. And it further confirms that dating and relationships are just incredibly elaborate emotional embezzlement schemes.

Serial Dating – often defined as that time in middle school when you would date a new person every couple of class periods – is the ability to date someone else the second your previous relationship ends. It is a cycle and doesn't have a clear end goal or any amount of emotional appeal whatsoever. Oftentimes, it is a covert operation that conceals the fact that what you're really after is quick and easy sex. Quick and easy sex wrapped up in a bow and called *a relationship*. And what is a relationship again? That's right: a scam. So, forget the emotional turn-around and get right back on that dating app bandwagon! In fact, I'll give you the biggest piece of advice you will have in your 20s, guaranteed:

- Create a DoodlePoll indicating the times in which you plan to be single. You can have the guys on your dating apps sign up for a time slot (no more than 2 hours, as little as 15 minutes!) to date you. Tell them they're allowed to spread the news of your new relationship to their friends and family – that way, when you break up with them and have a new guy within seconds, their friends and family will give them the comfort you never did.

Level 1: Dating Apps

- First, download a dating app; any will do.
- Next, think of a bio (short for "biography") for your dating profile. Make it represent you, or maybe not!
- A third piece of advice!

Level 2: The Perfect 1st Date

- Once you've filled out your dating profile, start chatting with other individuals.
- Avoid people who have the brainpower of a 5 year old. They're identifiable by how dull their responses are.
- Plan the perfect first date!

Level 3: Rinse & Repeat

- Rinse & Repeat the first two levels. Make it a game!
- Turn to the 'Ancient Middle School Courtship System of Hyperspeed Serial Dating'.
- Create a DoodlePoll to plan all of your dates.

Figure 5.2

However, don't forget why you're reading this chapter in the first place: because dating is fake and makes no sense whatsoever. That's why I'm ultimately proposing that none of us date each other anymore. It's over, y'all! It's cancelled! It's 2020, for crying out loud!

One time I went to a club. A stranger came up to me and the guy standing next to me. He asked us, "How long have you two been together?" Before me and the guy could explain that we don't even know each other, I replied, "Two years." Then me and my new boyfriend of two years, apparently, proceeded to pretend that we were in a bona fide long-term relationship, and none of it mattered! Now THAT'S a metaphor. That's the crutch of this philosophy. You can look at any single human being and decide right then and there exactly how long you have been dating, and whether or not you *are* dating. And guess what: none of it matters at all! So, why don't we cut the bullshit and move on to more important things? Like technological singularity or planting trees? Surely, we could be using our energy a lot more wisely than this.

Pivot to Vulnerability
Learning to Take Off the Mask and Own Your True Self While Leaning into the Discomfort of Shame & Truth

"Mask Off." – Future

Being vulnerable is difficult and a practice. As Brené Brown says, "Vulnerability vulnerability vulnerability!" I want to take some time to be open and vulnerable with you and share my journey to inspire your truth. But first, I have to ask: Are you ready to be vulnerable? Are you ready to take off the shield and run headfirst into the arena of discomfort? Are your ready to lean into the difficulties of a vulnerable life free of shame? If you answered vulnerably to any of these questions, you are ready to dive in! Ney, lean in!

The first step in being vulnerable is learning to take off the mask. We all wear masks, and while they are functional, they hide our true selves. To embrace who we are, we must lean into our mask and take it off. A great practice to incorporate daily is standing in your truth. This means embracing your shame and showing up. Taking ownership of this truth eventually results in the mask being shed and your shame being let go. This work is difficult! But with practice and mindfulness, you can vulnerably vulnerable your mask off in no time!

The second step towards vulnerability is leaning into the discomfort of shame and entering the arena of owning our truth. This is especially difficult if we are still wearing our mask, so I hope you shed that. By making boundaries and embracing fear we can destroy shame, and by destroying shame we show true courage. This courage allows us to open ourselves to vulnerability and our truth. This connection is difficult at first, but these boundaries and vulnerable acceptance of our flaws allow us to show up and be seen.

I feel vulnerable even making it this far, so I certainly hope you are leaning into the discomfort of this truth. But I do sense – because of my empath qualities – that you may have some objections. You fear vulnerability hangovers, the greatest risk of embracing our truth and taking risks. This occurs when we share our truths with one another and feel shame about our vulnerability. How do we overcome this? The answer is really simple and courageous: Lean into the discomfort of vulnerability and take off your mask! Once you are able to own your story and truth, you will feel vulnerable enough that your vulnerability hangover will create its own boundaries and begin to develop its own truth.

One of the most important steps in finding the courage to lean into our truth and take ownership of our vulnerability is to hold our shame close to us and enter the arena with openness and vulnerability. Once we reach this step, we are able to feel the vulnerability surge and the truth become exposed through the gaping mouth of our mask. Don't worry, this part is difficult. That's ok. Lean in so deep and hard into the arena that your empathy aura triples, and the shackles of shame become vulnerable. This will allow you to be seen in your boundaries!

We have done a lot of work here, so I want to allow us to pivot to time for self-care. Please go lean into that really quick. We have more work to do! P.S., my empath aura is picking up some discomfort and shame that I want to address. Moisturizing face masks are still masks, so you should create boundaries and shed those too. That's one thing we don't want to take ownership of! This also includes Halloween masks. Remember, this is the first step, folks. As a strong Texas girl, I know that Halloween is normal.

I've felt that shame, but if we lean in hard enough, we can embrace our truth.

As we continue our journey, I want to do a check in. I know you may be feeling imposter syndrome right now. *How can I embrace my truth with the exploration of vulnerability when shame seeps into my truth?* This is easier said than done, but we must lean into the discomfort of the work and authentically embrace all of our vulnerability. We have to stop this shame cycle! By entering our space and creating boundaries against this shame, we are able to validate our truth and lean into the arena of courage. Taking ownership of this allows us to be in a space of vulnerability and truth and vulnerability.

Circling back, Vulnerability Vulnerability Vulnerability Vulnerability Vulnerability

Vulnerability Vulnerability Vulnerability
Vulnerability Vulnerability Vulnerability
Vulnerability Vulnerability Vulnerability
Vulnerability Vulnerability Vulnerability
Vulnerability Vulnerability Vulnerability
Vulnerability Vulnerability Vulnerability
Vulnerability Vulnerability Vulnerability
Vulnerability Vulnerability Vulnerability
Vulnerability Vulnerability Vulnerability
Vulnerability Vulnerability Vulnerability
Vulnerability Vulnerability Vulnerability
Vulnerability Vulnerability Vulnerability
Vulnerability Vulnerability Vulnerability
Vulnerability Vulnerability Vulnerability
Vulnerability Vulnerability Vulnerability
Vulnerability Vulnerability Vulnerability
Vulnerability Vulnerability Vulnerability
Vulnerability Vulnerability.

Vulnerability Vulnerability Vulnerability
Vulnerability Vulnerability Vulnerability
Vulnerability Vulnerability Vulnerability
Vulnerability Vulnerability Vulnerability
Vulnerability Vulnerability Vulnerability

Vulnerability Vulnerability Vulnerability
Vulnerability Vulnerability Vulnerability
VulnerabilityVulnerability Vulnerability
Vulnerability Vulnerability Vulnerability
Vulnerability Vulnerability Vulnerability
Vulnerability Vulnerability Vulnerability
Vulnerability Vulnerability Vulnerability
Vulnerability Vulnerability Vulnerability
Vulnerability Vulnerability shame
Vulnerability Vulnerability Vulnerability
Vulnerability Vulnerability Vulnerability
Vulnerability Vulnerability Vulnerability
Vulnerability Vulnerability Vulnerability
Vulnerability Vulnerability Vulnerability
Vulnerability Vulnerability Vulnerability
Vulnerability Vulnerability Vulnerability.

Vulnerability Vulnerability Vulnerability
Vulnerability Vulnerability Vulnerability
Vulnerability Vulnerability Vulnerability
Vulnerability Vulnerability Vulnerability
Vulnerability Vulnerability Vulnerability
Vulnerability Vulnerability Vulnerability
Vulnerability Vulnerability Vulnerability

Vulnerability Vulnerability Vulnerability
Vulnerability Vulnerability Vulnerability
Vulnerability Vulnerability Vulnerability
Vulnerability Vulnerability Vulnerability
Vulnerability Vulnerability Vulnerability
Vulnerability Vulnerability Vulnerability
Vulnerability Vulnerability Vulnerability
Vulnerability Vulnerability Vulnerability
Vulnerability Vulnerability Vulnerability
Vulnerability Vulnerability Vulnerability
Vulnerability Vulnerability Vulnerability
Vulnerability Vulnerability Vulnerability
Vulnerability.

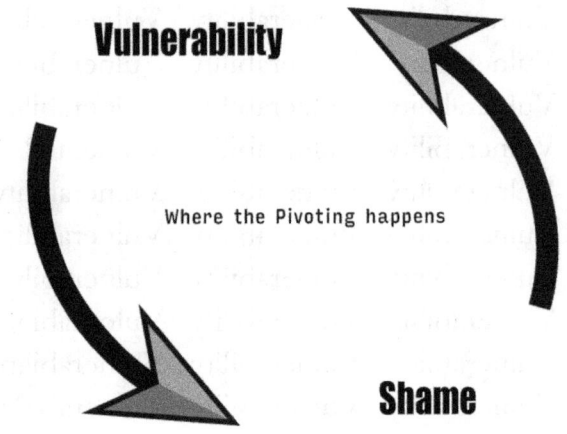

Figure 6.1

Thank y'all for allowing me the space to lean into my journey and take ownership of my truth. These masks are not for us to hold onto, and I want to be vulnerable here and say I am so grateful for you. You can embrace your story and create the boundaries against shame too. I know you can. You can embark on the adventure away from shame and enter the arena and vulnerable all over me. Take my hand as we journey to the Temple of Truth and sacrifice our first born at the Alter of Discomfort so the High-Priestess Brené Brown will end our shame cycle!!

BONUS CONTENT!
Fun Leadership Activities!

"Leadership: The action of taking multiple different personality assessments that each explain why you're better than everyone else." – The Dictionary, probably

Guess what. We're gonna teach you how to be a leader! Leadership is all about finding out if your personality even is, and like what. It's also all about making goals, figuring out your color, and being your very own CEO: Chief Emotional Officer™. If you think enough about it, your body is like a Corporation, and you're running it! And you should run it like a well-oiled machine, instead of into the ground like you usually do. Take notes!

Throughout this section, we provide you with fun leadership activities that help you understand the type of leader you are, and why you should be the one yelling at a group of people you get to call your inferiors. We also provide you with the tools to achieve your dreams of being better than other people, dominating your emotional baggage, and discovering how to give your personality a color (required for leadership roles, apparently). You'll find the following activities:

- DUMB Goals!
- Colored Leadership!
- Emotional Intelligence!

Feel free to rip out the pages! Like, any of the pages. Destroy this book, please.

Get DUMB!

First of all, what is DUMB? You, of course! Ha-ha, we're just kidding around. DUMB is an acronym you can use to guide your goal setting to ensure that your dreams are clear and reachable.

- **D**escribe (the goal)
- **U**tilize (the network)
- **M**easure (the quantities)
- **B**uild (the steps)

Do you have shivers too? I can already feel my dreams coming true, and I haven't even done anything! Before we give you the tools, we'll give you an example on the next page.

Here is the DUMB Goals activity sheet the authors of this book completed before writing it:

DUMB Goals!

D: Describe the goal. What exactly do you want to accomplish, and why? Manifest!

We want to write a really great book that not only helps other people, but more importantly helps us by getting us a lot of money so we can buy things like fall-themed items from discount grocery stores.

U: Utilize the network. Who can help you achieve this goal, and how? Connections!

We know a really stupid publishing house that will honestly accept any book without even reading the manuscript, so probably that. Also, our 97-year-old aunt gave us $200 each for the labor costs.

M: Measure the quantities. How long will it take? What will you need? Results!

Uhh… It'll probably take 5 days to write — how hard can writing a book be? It'll only be, like, 100 pages long. We both get so bored when a book decides to be more than 100 pages long. It's unnecessary.

B: Build the steps. How can it be broken down into smaller goals? Construct!

We will take turns writing a chapter until there are 6 chapters. We will consult with LinkedIn on the best self-help advice possible! We will also read Self-Help books from famous gurus like Adam Grant.

DUMB Goals!

D: Describe the goal. What exactly do you want to accomplish, and why? Manifest!

_____
_____
_____

U: Utilize the network. Who can help you achieve this goal, and how? Connections!

_____
_____
_____

M: Measure the quantities. How long will it take? What will you need? Results!

_____
_____
_____

B: Build the steps. How can it be broken down into smaller goals? Construct!

_____
_____
_____

Some Colors Are Just Better Than Others!

We've heard it time and time again: some colors are the cream of the crop, and some colors are just plain old flops! Like blue.

Anyway, on the next page, you'll fill out a questionnaire that will assess which color your leadership aura is. But be careful! This will decide your fate, making the difference between you becoming the next President of the United States of America or America's Next Top UGLY!

The available colors are:

- **Red:** You're doing amazing
- **Yellow:** Maybe try harder
- **Blue:** Seek help
- **Green:** Barely noticeable

Color by Leadership! Questionnaire

1. When you take a shit, how do you normally feel?
A. Good   B. Fantastic   C. Shitty   D. What?

2. A server says, "Enjoy your meal!" What do you say?
A. "Thanks!"   B. "You too!"   C. "No!"   D. "What?"

3. You're playing Putt-Putt – which place do you get?
A. 1st B. 2nd C. Last   D. I have absolutely no friends

4. Who is your favorite John?
A. Cena   B. F Kennedy   C. Stamos   D. 3:16

5. How often did you get bullied in high school?
A. Constantly   B. Frequently   C. Never   D. I Bullied

6. Would you ever sleep with your Professor?
A. What kind of que-   B. Yes!   C. No!   D. [redacted]

7. Would you give this book a positive review if we paid you $20?
A. Absolutely not

8. What is your go-to Instagram Filter?
A. Clarendon   B. Juno   C. I don't have Instagram
D. I've been missing for 15 years

9. [input question number 9]
A. I think you forg-   B. Idk how to answer this
C. This questionnaire is useless   D. 7

Color by Leadership!
Instructions

Now that you've completed the questionnaire, here is what you're going to do:

- Add up how many times you answered "A", how many times you answered "B", how many times you answered "C", and how many times you answered "D."
- Write those numbers down on individual pieces of paper, making sure they correspond with the letter.
- Pick one of the four following colors to write down next to each number: Red, Yellow, Blue, Green.
- Throw the pieces of paper into a bag and shake it for at least 3 minutes.
- Spin around in a circle with the bag in your hand 15 times, and then jump up and down 15 more times. Then do both motions together 15 final times.
- Once dizzy, open up the bag and randomly pick out just one piece of paper.

The piece of paper you obtain will tell you your Leadership Aura Color! Follow along on the next page to understand what your color means about your leadership style.

Color by Leadership! Assessment

RED: You are amazing. Truly amazing. You're doing amazing, and you're bringing amazing. Each person you interact with – day in and day out – falls in love with you 20 times over. Due to this innate ability to swoon others, you are built to be a Leader. You most likely governed an organization back in school, you always command your office at work, and you will go down as one of the most influential people on the planet.

YELLOW: Oof – you were *this* close to getting everything you ever wanted. Every word you want to say is always on the tip of your tongue. You'd be the best Leader on the block if only someone would give you a chance. But they never will, unfortunately. You continue to try harder, hoping that one day things will get better. All the way up until your death, which will be from natural causes – nothing to write home about.

BLUE: You need a therapist. No, seriously, you need psychological help beyond what this book can provide. Instead of completing this activity, you could've been working on yourself and fixing your flaws. But per usual, you avoid that. You make people's lives a little bit worse each and every time you talk. You're, like, the antithesis of a Leader.

GREEN: Oh, sorry I didn't see you there. What? You've worked here for how long? 15 years! Damn, I truly don't recognize you, or your name. Are you sure you're not pulling my leg? Hold on, let me get some coworkers over here. Hey guys, do you know this employee? That's what I said! Sorry dude, maybe next time.

Emotion: Not Just an Album by Carly Rae Jepsen!

Emotions. What are they?! Good question, but also bad. The correct question is: How are they? We often ask people *how* they're feeling, but we never stop to consider how our emotions might be feeling. In fact, our emotions have emotions, too! And checking in on our emotions' emotions… now that's Emotional Intelligence!

Ever heard of Empathy? More like Entropy. Your empathy is probably feeling pretty neglected and chaotic right now. You better take our Emotional Intelligence Exam (EIE) and our supplemental psychological evaluation: Intuition Ovulation (IO).

When combined, the EIEIO is effective at not only quantifying your level of emotional awareness, but also helping us data mine your emotional processes in order to provide you with the tools needed to be a great leader! But what exactly do these tests do?

The EIE is a set of 3 scenarios that provoke emotional responses, all of which implore you to provide open-ended statements on how you felt while reading them. <u>WARNING</u>: Do not take this exam lightly. Write down exactly how you felt in the answer box, or you're only cheating yourself. And your emotions!

The IO is a DIY, at-home method we invented for the everyday person! It requires equipment you need to buy, but that will be explained later. This method will discover if the Intuition Center of your brain is currently Ovulating. That's right – women's ovaries aren't the only things that Ovulate! So do our emotions.

Let's get into it!

Emotional Intelligence Exam
EIE Scenario 1

Scenario:

You're walking along a railroad track at midnight on November 4th, 2010. Your mother has always told you not to explore this area at night because of an increase in mysterious murders that have been happening over the past two years. As you come up to a crossing in two separate tracks, a train beams its light in your direction. Suddenly, you see a family of 12 tied to the first set of tracks, but they're, like, totally fine with it. They all want to die, and this is the happiest day of their life. It's so weird. Anyway, on the second set of tracks, you see one person: the love of your life, Todd. Todd also wants to die, and he promises you he will make love to you in the afterlife if you pull the Conductor Switch so that the train runs over him instead. Both Todd and the Family of 12 are begging you to kill them. Which do you kill?

Statement:

_____
_____
_____
_____
_____
_____
_____
_____
_____

Emotional Intelligence Exam
EIE Scenario 2

Scenario:

Okay, so you chose to kill Todd because the sweet promise of his ghost dick was too good to pass up. Immediately after pulling the switch, you threw yourself down on the tracks to die next to Todd to get laid faster (you're still a virgin). But now Todd is totally blowing you off in the afterlife! What gives?! You ask your ghost therapist for advice, because you thought this deal with Todd was pretty iron-clad. I mean, he seemed super eager to die, and he wouldn't just give an empty promise like that – would he? Sheryl (ghost therapist) suggests you just move on, but what does she know? She's never felt the love you feel for Todd, and she died by slipping on water and falling out of a window. Lame. Do you listen to Sheryl and move on, or pursue Todd's ghost dick until the end of ghost time?

Statement:

_____
_____
_____
_____
_____
_____
_____
_____
_____
_____

Emotional Intelligence Exam
EIE Scenario 3

Scenario:

Uh-oh, we have a problem. That family of 12 finally died and now they're haunting you! Like a meta-ghost-haunting, somehow? Weird. This would be fine and all, but you still have a mission: to get laid! Every time you try to hit on Todd, the ghost family shows up and mocks you for having tiny tits. They say things like, "How can you even compete with Ghost Stacy when you have tiny baby doodie tits like that??" and "You should've killed us that day, fart wad." You're starting to think your ghost therapist was right: you should move on from Todd and try to find happiness as a virgin through hobbies. Maybe brunch-hopping? But this ghost family is pretty annoying, nonetheless. Do you offer them a ritual sacrifice to leave you alone, or just deal with being meta-haunted forever?

Statement:

_____
_____
_____
_____
_____
_____
_____
_____
_____

Intuition Ovulation
IO Kit Instructions

Is the Intuition Center of your brain in Ovulation? We're about to find out! The Do-It-Yourself, At-Home IO Kit finally gives you a way to know if your Emotions are ready to be penetrated by Intelligence. This only happens once a month, so here's how you can find out.

What you'll need:
- Duct Tape
- Water Hose (2x)
- Garage Sale Stickers (pack of 150)
- A Fishbowl
- An Imagination!

Instructions:
- Drill two holes into the fishbowl and then put it on your head. Seal the bottom around your neck with duct tape.
- Attach one end of the water hoses to your house water system, and the other end to the holes in your fishbowl helmet. Turn the water on.
- Place the garage sale stickers all over your body, haphazardly.

And that's it! The longer you can hold out doing this, the more your intuition is ovulating! It takes an incredibly intelligent person to outlast 3 hours!

Emotional Intelligence Score: Putting the EIEIO Together

I know what you're thinking: *How have I never thought of doing these assessments before! They're so smart and obvious! Heath and Austin must be absolute geniuses. I owe them my life, and I cannot wait to offer them whatever they need until the end of time. I agree to enter into contractual obligation to wash their feet with my hair WHENEVER they ask. Thank you, Self-Help gods!*

Calm down. While we've been told that many times, we just want to help people. With real, bona fide science. So let's get into it!

In order to get your final EIEIO score, you'll take your answers from the Emotional Intelligence Exam and the final amount of time you were able to spend conducting the Intuition Ovulation assessment. You'll multiply the two together and then divide that answer by 52. Then, you'll take 4% of 10% of that answer, and convert it into a fraction over the number 9. Don't worry – when you think you've done the algorithm wrong, you're usually right. Then you'll take that final answer and add two '0's to the end of it, before finally drawing a graph of each common denominator that can be divided by 3 within the number itself. The last thing you'll do is say the number into your bathroom mirror 3 times in a row, and then wash your hands.

We sincerely hope this helps you and brings you peace and happiness.

Empirical Figures Index!
1.1 – 6.1

"Unless you put your content into a neat graph, no one is listening!" – Mark

Did you love our book? Do you want all of the neat formulas we created compiled in one convenient location at the end of the book? Well... turn the page. WOAH, now how did that happen?! It looks like your wish came true ☺ Don't spend all of that good luck in one place, champ.

Figure 1.1

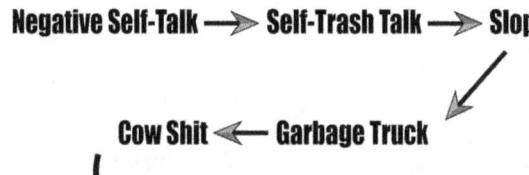

Figure 1.2

Reaching Dank Scum Existence

"I really wish someone would date me and have wild animal sex with me, but I am too ugly." **'A'** variable	"I hate my ugly ass with a passion and everyone should hate me just as much if not more and I will most certainly never get laid in the butt." **'B'** variable
"My life has no purpose, I have no connection to anyone, and I must live out my wasted self until I face a boring death." **'C'** variable	"LOL FUCK IT IM UGLY AF AND REPULSIVE SUCK MY NASTY PEEN." **'D'** variable
<u>'Dark Scam Existence'</u> Model $A \to B \to C$	<u>'Dank Scum Existence'</u> Model $A \to D \to @ \to \% \to :p \to G$

Figure 2.1

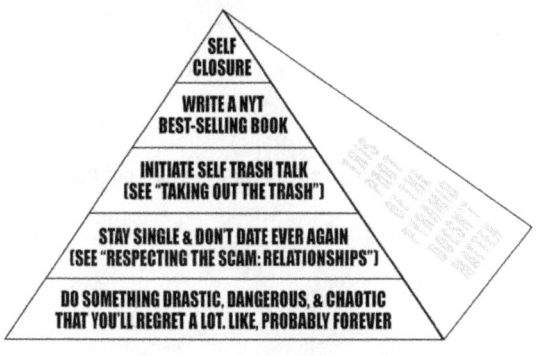

Figure 3.1

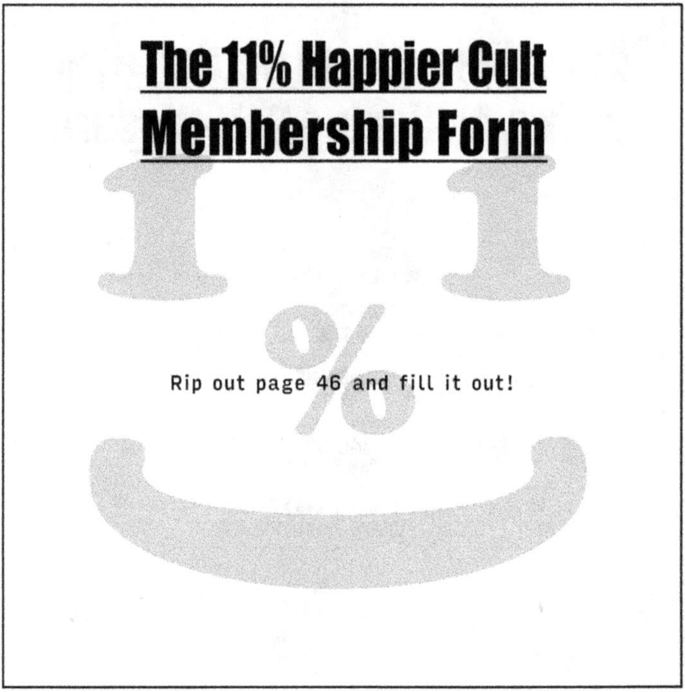

The 11% Happier Cult Membership Form

Rip out page 46 and fill it out!

Figure 4.1

Live, Laugh Love:
It's The LLLaw!

Dictum Primus: LIVE
To reach the enlightened state of LIVE, simply don't die! Follow these techniques to not die: NEVER leave your house, get a sword and surveillance equipment, alert emergency services all the time, eat healthy meals and exercise, and build a bunker!

Dictum Dos: LAUGH
Through a complex algorithm, figure out the exact quantity and quality of LAUGHter you need. While full belly laughter is superior to the chuckle, there is a link to cancer with hardcore laughter. It's best to use SL: Standard Laughter. Now do this constantly forever!

Dicktum Threesome: LOVE
X=Y   Y=ABC   ABC=WQ+JKLMAO^4   ▦▦▦▦▦▦ - Q= <(._.<)
Quadratic Formula of Pie * 11   **10=LOVE**

Figure 5.1

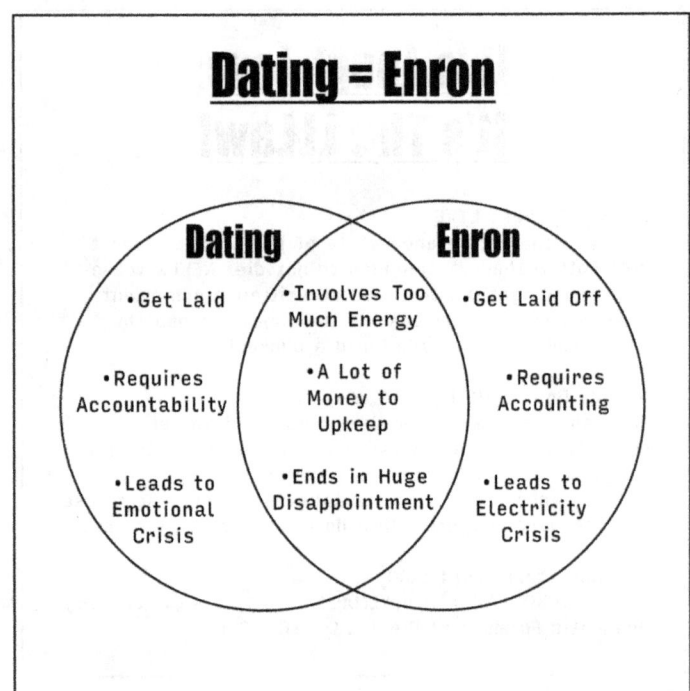

Figure 5.2

The Levels of Scam Dating

Level 1:
Dating Apps

- First, download a dating app; any will do.

- Next, think of a bio (short for "biography") for your dating profile. Make it represent you, or maybe not!

- A third piece of advice!

Level 2:
The Perfect 1st Date

- Once you've filled out your dating profile, start chatting with other individuals.

- Avoid people who have the brainpower of a 5 year old. They're identifiable by how dull their responses are.

- Plan the perfect first date!

Level 3:
Rinse & Repeat

- Rinse & Repeat the first two levels. Make it a game!

- Turn to the 'Ancient Middle School Courtship System of Hyperspeed Serial Dating'.

- Create a DoodlePoll to plan all of your dates.

Figure 6.1

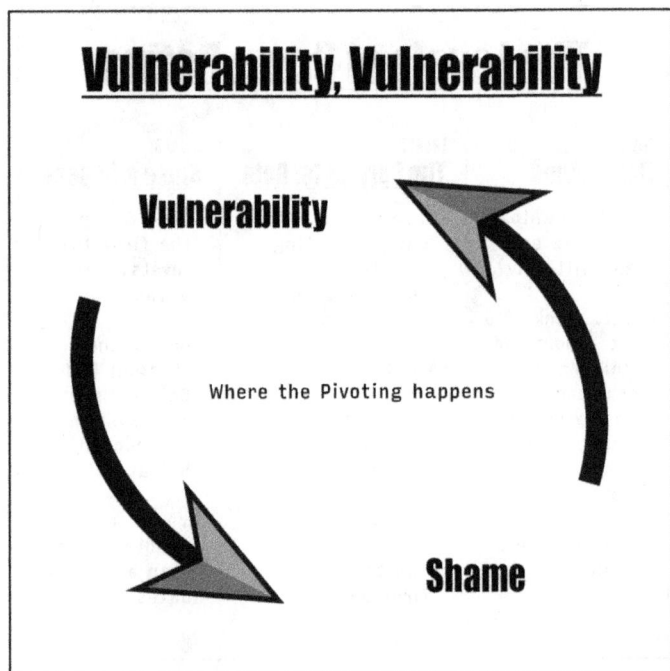

ABOUT THE AUTHORS

Austin Robinson holding his Canadian citizenship & some corn

Austin J. Robinson is a self - proclaimed "LinkedInfluencer." He practices the radical art of Self-Help, despite all odds, and believes everyone holds the potential to buy this book and change their life. He leads by the philosophy of Revolutionary Failure™.

Heath Fowler wearing a cowboy hat while shopping at Cabela's

Heath Fowler is a scholar at the Institute of Life and has dedicated his existence to fulfilling others. He enjoys meditating in his free time, as well as traveling. When not meditating or traveling, you can find him meditating or traveling. He's also a self-described "foodie."

www.ingramcontent.com/pod-product-compliance
Lightning Source LLC
Chambersburg PA
CBHW061332040426
42444CB00011B/2886